Christmas 2004

To Sophia from
Nana - Papa

A Christmas Journey

Thanks to Jonnie B, Malcolm Down, Phil Grundy, Julie Clayden, Jo Poole, Peter and Veronica Batsford, John Nicholson and Mum

A Christmas Journey

From creation to the Savior's birth

SUSIE POOLE

STANDARD PUBLISHING
CINCINNATI, OHIO

Christmas Is Coming

God loves light. He always has. It was the first thing he created and it was good.

And now we're getting ready for Christmas, and the streets look so beautiful as they sparkle with colored lights. Soon our Christmas tree will glow cheerily through the window, heavy with twinkling lights, ornaments, and ribbons.

At home, we light pretty candles and put them on a high shelf where they light up the whole room. As the flames dance this way and that, we remember the time, long ago, when God sent his Christmas light into the world.

Here our Christmas journey begins…

The Journey Begins

When everything was dark, empty, and cold, God decided that the time had come to create a beautiful world, full of his light. So he used his magnificent voice and spoke the words, "Let there be light." And there was!

God separated the light from the darkness. He called the light "day" and darkness "night," and in doing so, he made the first day.

Now God had *many* creation ideas buzzing around in his head, so next he made the sky, the sea, and the land. Then he filled them up with every kind of living thing, from the most enormous elephant to the teeny-weeniest turtle.

But God wasn't finished making his beautiful, brand new world. He said, "Let us make someone extra special in our own image. Let us make people!" And so he did.

First God made a man, called Adam. Soon God decided it wasn't good for Adam to live his life alone, so he created a lovely woman, called Eve, to be Adam's wife.

Then God gave Adam and Eve a beautiful garden to live in. There they ruled over the animals, ate delicious food, and—best of all—walked and talked with their wonderful daddy—God!

The First Sin

God wanted Adam and Eve to enjoy his creation, but he warned them not to eat the fruit from one tree in the middle of the garden. If they ate fruit from that tree, they would certainly die.

Everything was perfect, until one day Satan came as a crafty snake to cause trouble for Adam and Eve. Slithering down the tree trunk, the snake told the first and biggest lie that has ever been told. "God doesn't mean it when he says you will die if you eat this fruit," said the snake. "Instead you will become as *clever* as him if you eat it."

Eve wanted to be clever, so she plucked a lovely piece of fruit from the tree and ate it. Eve handed some to Adam, who also ate the fruit. Suddenly the day grew dark.

Adam and Eve knew they had made a horrible mistake. By choosing to disobey God, Adam and Eve brought sin into the world.

They hoped God would not see what they had done, but he knew everything that had happened. With a sad and heavy heart, God sent Adam and Eve away from the garden forever. Adam and Eve cried. God cried too.

God Has a Plan

Everything had changed. Away from the garden, Adam and Eve felt cold. So God made them clothes from animal skins to keep them warm.

Adam and Eve had lots of children. After many years, they filled the whole earth. Sadly, they soon became full of hate and forgot what it was like to have God's wonderful light living inside them. But God still loved them, and he had a plan to bring his light back.

God's plan was like a big jigsaw puzzle. At the right times, he gave new puzzle pieces to men and women who loved him and longed for his light. He gave one piece to a man called Isaiah. This is what God said to him …

People who are walking in the darkness will see a great light. For a child will be born and he will rule the world, bringing peace, fairness, and goodness . . . He will be called "God with us."

Unexpected News

Many people tried to guess what the puzzle pieces meant. Some put the pieces together in the wrong order. Nobody could agree on what God would do.

Zechariah and Elizabeth were an elderly couple who spent their lives loving God, longing for his light, and praying for a family. But now they were much too old to have a baby.

Zechariah was a priest who served in the temple in Jerusalem. While on special duty one day, a miracle happened. A bright light filled the temple and in the middle of it stood a mighty gleaming angel named Gabriel.

"Greetings!" said the angel. "God is going to give you the son you have always longed for. You will call him John. He will have the job of getting people ready to meet the Savior King, the one who will bring God's light back into the world."

Zechariah was amazed. Perhaps that is why he doubted the angel's words at first. But asking the angel if he had mixed up his message was a big mistake. To prove it was true, the angel took away Zechariah's voice until the day the baby was born.

Zechariah and Elizabeth now had plenty to do. They wanted to be ready for this special baby.

Mary Is Chosen

In the village of Nazareth, Elizabeth's young relative, Mary, was making preparations of her own. She was soon to be married to Joseph.

As Mary swept and baked, washed and mended, she sang thank-you songs to God. She had no idea that God had been looking everywhere for a heart as beautiful as hers. He had chosen her for a very special task.

That night, heaven hushed its singing and the angel Gabriel visited earth once more. He was bringing God's most important message to Mary.

"You are very special and God is with you," whispered Gabriel. "He will surprise you with a son and you will call him Jesus. His kingdom will rule for ever and ever. The Spirit of God will rest on you and your baby will be the perfect Son of God."

Then Gabriel told Mary all about Zechariah and Elizabeth's miracle baby. "You see?" he smiled. "Nothing is impossible for God!"

"Yes," replied Mary, "I do see. Let everything you have said happen to me."

Songs of Joy

The next day, Mary quickly packed her things and joined some travelers journeying to Elizabeth's village in Judea.

"Is anybody home?" called Mary as she arrived at the house. At the sound of these words, the baby in Elizabeth's tummy leaped and wriggled. This baby knew that somebody special had arrived.

Elizabeth was so happy that she laughed, cried, and sang a new song…

"You are so blessed,
More blessed than the rest,
Your baby has caused me to sing.
But who am I that you should come
To me, with such great news to bring."

Mary sang too…

"I'm dancing and singing the song of my God,

I'm happy as happy could be.

God looked through the earth for a woman to bless,

And look who he chose, he chose me.

The weak will be strong,

The poor will be rich,

The proud won't be proud any more.

He promised to give us this wonderful gift,

Now it's waiting for us at the door."

The Birth of John

While Elizabeth's baby was growing inside her, Zechariah was unable to speak. But finally the child was born. Soon the time came to name the baby. Zechariah recalled what the angel had said, and motioned for a writing tablet. He wrote down the words, "His name is John." Immediately, Zechariah could speak again.

"God, you are fantastic!" cried Zechariah. "You are giving us One who will show your light in the darkness. You have remembered your promises to us. And my son, John, has arrived first to make sure that everyone is ready to meet the Savior who is coming."

After John was born, it was time for Mary to leave. With wonder in her heart, she kissed baby John, said good-bye to Elizabeth and Zechariah, and began the long journey home.

Mary and Joseph

Now that Mary had returned to Nazareth, it was time to tell Joseph about all the amazing events that had taken place. First she told him about Zechariah and Elizabeth's baby. Joseph thought this was wonderful news and clapped with joy. Then Mary told Joseph that she also was expecting a baby.

This, Joseph decided, was not good news. He did not believe that Mary's baby had been put in Mary's tummy by God.

Joseph was so upset that he no longer wanted Mary to be his wife. She was heartbroken.

But that night, an angel visited Joseph in a dream and told him that the baby really was God's Son, and that he would be named Jesus. Joseph was so happy that he brought Mary home to be his wife after all.

Journey to Bethlehem

Many months had passed and the baby was soon to be born. Mary's tummy was large and sore. Joseph told her that the Roman rulers had ordered everyone to travel to their family town to sign their names in a big book. Mary was not happy because they had to go all the way to Bethlehem.

They packed their clothes, strips of cloths for the baby, and plenty of food and water. God was with them, and he smiled on them all the way.

When Mary and Joseph arrived in Bethlehem, it was bustling with visitors. Leaving Mary under the shade of a palm tree, Joseph set off through the crowds to find somewhere to stay. Tired and uncomfortable, Mary waited and watched.

By the time Joseph returned, Mary was crying. So Joseph held her gently and told her about the kind innkeeper who had taken pity on them and offered his stable. At that moment it seemed just perfect.

Angels and Shepherds

On the hillside outside Bethlehem, a group of shepherds were keeping warm around a fire. They were talking and laughing together after a hard day of protecting their sheep. But as their laughter rolled across the hilltop, a strange light appeared above them. Soon it was shining all around. When the shepherds saw a mighty angel in the night sky, they were terrified.

"Don't be afraid," the angel told them. "I have great news to tell you. A king has been born in Bethlehem, and he is called Jesus. This is what you should look for—a baby wrapped in strips of cloth, lying in a manger."

The sky seemed to explode as a host of angels began swooping and singing, "Glory to God in the highest, and peace on earth to men and women, the ones God loves."

The light faded and the songs became only a whisper. The shepherds helped each other to their feet and began to stumble, then walk, and then run toward the village of Bethlehem.

Sharing the News

"God's eyes are on me!" shouted one of the shepherds. "God is with us!" sang another. As they ran, they began to laugh. Joy bubbled up inside them like a mountain stream.

Soon they found the stable where the baby Jesus was sleeping. As they walked through the door, they were overwhelmed. There was Jesus, their newborn king. They fell to their knees and worshiped him. Jesus would give them a new start. He had turned their darkness into light.

It was still dark when the shepherds left the stable, but they didn't leave quietly. They laughed and sang praises to God as they returned to their sheep. As they sang, Bethlehem woke from its sleep. Leaning out of windows and standing in doorways, people heard the good news about Jesus and shared the shepherds' joy.

Simeon's Blessing

A few weeks later, Mary and Joseph took Jesus to visit the temple in Jerusalem.

There was an old man in Jerusalem named Simeon, who had spent his whole life watching, waiting, and praying for God to send his light back into the world. On that same day, God told Simeon to visit the temple, because something wonderful was waiting for him there.

As Simeon entered the crowded temple courts, he saw Joseph carrying a basket with two doves for an offering, and Mary holding baby Jesus. As Simeon took the baby and cradled him in his arms, his heart was bursting with thanks to God.

Simeon said, "Now I have seen with my own eyes the light that will change the world. At last I can die in peace."

Then Simeon told Mary and Joseph that Jesus would someday show people that their lives needed to change, and that this would make people angry. In fact, just by hearing about Jesus' birth, someone was already very angry.

A Wicked King

King Herod had no idea about Jesus' birth until a group of wise men arrived in Jerusalem. "Where is the baby king?" they asked. "We saw his star in the east and have come to worship him."

King Herod was proud and evil. He would not allow some baby to be as important as him. No way! Long ago, God had spoken about a Savior King being born in Bethlehem. Herod wondered if this baby was the one.

So the king sent the wise men toward Bethlehem. "Go and search everywhere for the baby," he said, "and when you find him, come back and tell me so that I can worship him, too."

This was untrue, of course. Herod did not want to worship Jesus at all.

Gifts for a King

The wise men followed the star again until it came to rest over a little house on the outskirts of Bethlehem. The wise men looked out of place in their beautiful, rainbow-colored clothes. But when they saw Jesus, they gladly knelt down and worshiped him.

Opening their treasure box, they presented baby Jesus with gifts of gold, frankincense, and myrrh. Each gift was like a story, telling something about who Jesus was and what he would do.

Gold was a very expensive gift that was fit for a king. Jesus was a king! What a lovely present.

Frankincense was a sweet-smelling perfume used to worship God. Jesus was God's Son! How clever of the wise men.

But myrrh? This was a spice used to prepare people for burial! Did the wise men really want Mary and Joseph to think about Jesus dying?

Escape to Egypt

As the wise men slept that night, they were warned in a dream not to return to Herod's palace. So they traveled home by a secret route.

When Herod realized that the wise men were not coming back to the palace to tell him where Jesus could be found, he was furious. They had tricked him! In his madness, he gave orders to kill every boy child in Bethlehem under two years old.

An angel came to Joseph in a dream and said, "Get up! Take Jesus and Mary and escape to Egypt. Stay there until I tell you to leave, because Herod wants to kill the child."

Joseph, Mary, and Jesus found safety in Egypt. There they lived under God's protection until Herod died. Then an angel appeared to Joseph once more in a dream and said, "Herod is dead. It's time to go home."

The Journey Ends

Our Christmas journey has come to an end. When they returned home, Mary and Joseph began their life as an ordinary little family—working, eating, and playing with their child. Angels no longer talked to them in their dreams and strange visitors did not pass by to worship Jesus.

In her heart, Mary remembered all the wonderful things that happened to Jesus and all that was said about him. There would be many difficult times ahead,

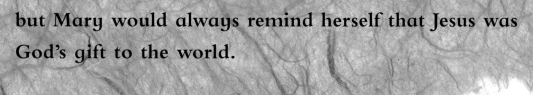

but Mary would always remind herself that Jesus was God's gift to the world.

And what a wonderful gift he is! There is so much to be enjoyed at Christmas. But when all the tree lights have been taken down and the parties have ended, Jesus will still be there—showing us God's love and his amazing light.

Thank you, Jesus.

GLOSSARY

ANGEL	*a messenger from God*
BETHLEHEM	*the town where Jesus was born*
BLESS	*speaking or doing good things for another person*
CREATION	*when God made the world*
GABRIEL	*the angel who announced that John and Jesus would be born*
GARDEN OF EDEN	*the place God made for Adam and Eve to live*
HEAVEN	*God's special place where everything is perfect*
ISAIAH	*a man who received a special message from God about Jesus*
JERUSALEM	*a very important city close to where Jesus lived*
JOHN	*the special son of Zechariah and Elizabeth*

MANGER	*where hay was put for the animals to eat*
MIRACLE	*something God does in an amazing or unexpected way*
NAZARETH	*the town where Joseph, Mary, and Jesus lived*
PRIEST	*a special temple worker who was in charge of worship and sacrifices*
SAVIOR	*someone who rescues people*
TEMPLE	*a building where people went to worship God*
WORSHIP	*the way we let God know how much we love him and thank him for what he has done*

A CHRISTMAS JOURNEY

Copyright © 2001, 2003 Susie Poole.

This edition published by Standard Publishing, Cincinnati, Ohio.

A division of Standex International Corporation. All rights reserved.

Sprout logo is a trademark of Standard Publishing. Printed in China.

ISBN: 0-7847-1461-4

Produced for Standard Publishing by Pupfish Limited.

www.pupfish.co.uk